Money Management

Become a Master in a Short Time on How to Create a Budget, Save Your Money and Get Out of Debt while Building your Financial Freedom

Volume 2

By

Income Mastery

Table of Contents

Introduction to Financial Freedom

It is extremely important to build a real budget, have a good attitude, get organized, have goals, and stay motivated. Now let us begin with the path to savings, the payment of our debts and financial freedom. In this book we will teach you how to pay your debts, save and build your financial freedom. We know it sounds complicated, but it's simpler than it sounds.

Let's start by thinking about what financial freedom is for you. What do you want to be financially free for? Do you want to be able to travel whenever you want? Do you want to be your own boss? Do you want to stop working regular office hours of nine to five every day? Do you want to be able to save to buy your apartment or house in cash? Think exactly what you want this financial freedom for and always keep it in mind. Use it as your mantra, remember and think about what you want to achieve every day. Visualize it, write it down, write it down in your diary, write it down in your diary, think about it and write it down every day and think about how you're going to make it. It is very important that we believe in ourselves and are determined and convinced that we are going to achieve it. The mentality is really important, we must be positive and we must know that we are going to achieve it, that the path is going to be a little complicated but that we will achieve it. We must always remain motivated and strive to accomplish what we set out to do.

Now that we know what we want to do and why we want to do it, that is, why we want this freedom, we will have a clearer idea of how and how much to save in our budget. The amount that we must keep will vary according to our objective, that is to say, the amount of savings that we must keep will have to be greater or less depending on what is going to be our objective.

Ten finds that we can achieve financial freedom in several ways, not only by saving more money, we can also generate more money. Do you know how? Keep reading that we will explain it with examples, pages and explain different easy and quick ways to get money in different ways, we can get separate jobs not necessarily in a shop or an office, we can also increase our income in another way.

Is it possible to enjoy your money by having money in the bank and paying all your debts? Of course, we can, can we achieve financial freedom and enjoy our money at the same time? The answer is also yes.

Do you know how to save? Have you ever taken a break before making a purchase? Has anyone taught you how to save? Do you know how to spend? These are fundamental questions we must ask ourselves in order to achieve financial freedom. It seems unreal the question of if we know how to spend, but the truth is that many times we spend on things we don't need, that we already have or that we will never use and we only buy them because we think they could be practical and could serve us at some point. Weird, isn't it? What are you spending on? Why do you have so many debts? These are key questions for changing our habits and becoming more aware of how we are handling our money. Knowing how to save and how to use our money and most of all our credit cards is of utmost importance. Do we really know how to use them? Do you know what the card is giving you as a benefit? Better yet, do you really know how much your credit card interest rate is or how much you have to pay for membership annually? Most people don't know this and this is vital in order to increase our income and have a balance.

Now how do we increase our income and get out of debt if we don't really know how much we earn and spend?

Let's start with the first and most important thing for the creation of our budget, this is the path to financial freedom. We need to do a meticulous financial analysis and really see how we are financially. This means, we must see what debts we have, no matter how small they are, no matter if we can postpone them, we must know what they are and put them in our budget. We must be truly honest with ourselves and review every detail. Let's start by actually calculating how much our income is. For this, we must know exactly what income we have, but we must do this realistically. Let's calculate how much our fixed monthly income is, don't forget that this income must be the same every month and must be fixed. We cannot count the money we think we are going to receive; it is always better to think that we are going to receive less instead of increasing this amount, in this way we can save what we have left to save it or for an emergency fund that is really important. Don't forget to deduct your taxes from your monthly and annual income.

Now we must continue to plan and review the following points, if we already know what our real monthly fixed income is, now we must know what we are spending and what type of expenses we are facing.

We must separate our expenses into two groups, let's start with our indispensable fixed expenses. These are the non-negotiable expenses for us, those that we need to live on, for example, the rent of our house or our apartment, the services that we must pay where we live such as the cost of water, electricity, our cell phone and/or landline, cable, food for our house, gas for our car in case we have one, our health insurance that is really important, among others. We must know how much these expenses are monthly because they are the first thing, we must pay; these are the living expenses that if or if we must pay.

On the other hand, we must also analyze expenditure which is not indispensable. Are there non-essential expenditure? What do we mean by this? Yes, for example, if we go out to work or go for a walk the amount of coffee we buy when we go out, the sandwich in the cafeteria, all the restaurants or delivery's we order when we are lazy cooking. Why do we say that these are expenses that are not indispensable? Because we can reduce them. For example, if you are consuming one coffee a day the five days of the week you are working and the coffee costs five dollars a day, a week is twenty-five dollars, a month is one hundred dollars, a year are one thousand two hundred dollars in coffee. Just as you read it, this is just one example of something that would help you reduce your non-essential expenses. For example, if you have Spotify Premium, if you have a Netflix account, you also have to pay a subscription. Let's say that between these two subscriptions you pay twenty dollars a month, in one year there are two hundred and forty dollars that you pay only in Netflix and Spotify. Add to that the thousand two hundred dollars of daily office coffee, you already have one thousand four hundred and forty dollars in expenses that you could avoid. Am I spending so much money when I go out or for my convenience? That's right. That's right. That's right.

Why are we talking about comfort? Because instead of listening to Spotify we can listen to music on other channels such as YouTube or we can even listen to music on Spotify but on the regular plan that has no cost. The same happens with Netflix, we can watch movies and series not only on Netflix, we can also watch them if we have cable in our house or we can search for different websites that have the same series and movies but have no cost. Of course, the difference is that in Netflix you enter and search for the series and to be able to search for it on a website you will take at least twenty minutes. Here we must make a rational analysis and remember that what we want is more important than that time spent looking for the film, that is, our financial freedom is priceless. We must concentrate on why we should save and why we are making these reductions in subscriptions.

Now, with the data of how much is our real income, not what we think we can earn but what we are actually earning monthly and already knowing how much our indispensable and non-essential expenses are, we must make the subtraction of our income minus our expenses. These numbers must be real in order to calculate this number correctly. We recommend that you look up last year's receipts to get an idea of how much you've spent and, more importantly, on what. This is going to cover us in case we have more consumptions and in case our account is the number that we have budgeted or less, we can save that money or we can destine it to the payment of our debts, that is to say, to the payment of capital of our debts to avoid having interests.

When you make a principal payment, rather than a general payment to that total amount, we avoid paying interest. When we have this calculation ready (our income minus our expenses) we can see how much deficit or surplus we have. After this, we only have to make a monthly budget to see how much we can spend on food, eating out, shopping, among others. In case we do not have a surplus, or we even lack a monthly amount to be able to pay all our debts, we must get and review which are the best options to increase our monthly income. We must know exactly what amount we must increase monthly to avoid falling into debt and pay everything in cash not to use the credit card.

The problem with using a credit card is that many times, or most times, we don't keep in mind how much interest we actually have to pay if we can't pay the full amount of our debt the previous month. Sometimes we go out and start paying small things with the credit card, which hurts us because sometimes we forget or do not pay the full amount then we end up paying many times almost double what we actually spent. Keep these little tips in mind so you can start making more conscious decisions.

Chapter I: Financial freedom

Now, how to achieve financial freedom? Let us remember that if we already have a monthly budget, we must respect it. It is often difficult to stay exactly within the numbers, but we must make every effort to do so. You'll see that once you begin to see your debts diminish and realize the amount of money, you're saving by not drinking a soda, coffee and eating a sandwich during work hours, you'll stop making it happy and look for ways to bring your food or even start taking your instant coffee to work. Of course, it won't taste like coffee in a cafeteria, but your savings account will thank you.

We must keep you focused and always keep in mind why and what we are saving for. If we lose sight of this, it is going to make everything more difficult, this usually happens when we have finished paying our debts, instead of saving, as we see a greater surplus in our savings account than we saw before we begin to spend it without realizing it. When we really rethink and return to the state of consciousness in our expenses that we had before, we realize how much we have spent and it is too late to recover it.

It is really important that we take into account that we must live within our means. Many times, we like to impress other people and for this reason we pay more than we should when we ask for the bill and we want to invite people, suddenly our boss or our colleagues, our family, among others. We do not realize that this is

12

hurting us, that we are not living within our means and that we do not have direction of our expenses, we are simply spending for the sake of spending and that is not good. In the end, we must understand that working more does not mean being debt free, just as having more income does not mean that we will be debt free. We must be aware of our income and of our expenses. What is the use of increasing our income by even 100%, that is, doubling our income if in the end we are also spending twice as much because we think we have money?

We need to be really careful and aware that we can save money, and that there are different types of savings accounts and even investment funds that generate more money because they pay more interest. In other words, money calls money, the more money we have and can save, the more money we can make. Curious, isn't it?

Chapter II: How can we increase our income?

In the following chapters we will show you how to increase our income in order to achieve financial freedom by increasing our income.

When doing your budget did you realize that you need more money to be able to pay your debts and to be able to save? Don't worry, there are many ways to earn more money apart from going to an office eight hours a day.

Let's start, the first and most obvious option is to ask for a raise in work. When to ask for a raise? If you have many years in the company, make an effort and do a good job, it could be a good time to ask for a raise. How to ask? We know that talking to your boss or the person in charge is a little complicated and can be uncomfortable. Before going to the office, check what your functions are, what you are doing in the company, your pending, additional tasks you must perform, the hours you work in the day, among others. Having this information updated and really reviewing what it is that you are doing and have done, is very important because you can also feel more comfortable asking for the increase to the company because you know what your value is, really, what your contribution is.

In addition to this, we might be asked about some of our functions that we don't know, don't remember, or we might think that some additional tasks that we perform are our functions and they are not. This will take you about ten minutes. If you're nervous, practice with a friend. We don't recommend that you talk to your colleagues about this, because you can generate envy and jealousy or a colleague could go ahead and talk to your boss and that's not the idea. It would be best to practice it with someone in your family or someone you trust. This will be better because you will feel more secure and the other person may also give you some idea of how to ask for it. You can measure your tone of voice and already go with a "speech" prepared of what it is that you are going to say. Also, between the two people may think of some questions that your boss might ask you and you could practice the answers that is what we recommend.

If your boss accepts the raise, it would be perfect if you don't work more hours and have this extra raise. Remember that once they accept your increase you will have to update your budget. Do not increase your expenses evidently, you must continue with your fixed expenses and continue reducing your additional expenses that are not necessary. We give you some examples, Netflix and Spotify, we know they help us make our lives more fun in the sense that we don't like to wait, we want to hear the song we like at that moment that's probably why we have Spotify Premium. Remember that these expenses, no matter how small they seem to you, add up, not only monthly but also annually. On the other hand, we like Netflix because we don't have to look for different alternatives on the internet to watch that movie or series that isn't on television. Now, let's remember that they both add up, if you pay 20 dollars a month between the two for example, it is one hundred and forty dollars annually and these are only two of the subscriptions we have, how many subscriptions do you have? That amount can be used to pay your debts, pay your mortgage or better yet, add it to your savings account, remember that the more money in that account the more interest you will have.

Continue to live as if you haven't received an increase, continue with your budget, don't modify it, just add that additional payment to your debts, your savings account or your emergency fund. Is it necessary to make this change and not have that payment? Yeah, it's really important to do this. Don't go into debt again! You are asking for this increase in order to be able to save and to be able to acquire your financial freedom. Don't forget it! It's very easy to lose what our goal is, so think every day about what you want to achieve and how you're going to achieve it, be aware of your purchases and your budget.

On the other hand, if we can't ask for a raise because we're very new, the company isn't having a good time or we just can't do it, we can look to evaluate our options. So, now, let's think, do you want to keep working in the same place? In case you like to work in an office but you know you won't be able to get a raise, you can start looking for another job that can pay you what you would need to be able to cover your debts, save, have an emergency fund and acquire an emergency fund.

Then start looking for jobs that fit you and your profile, check where they fit, whether they fit closer to where you're living or farther away. Why is it so important to evaluate this point? Because you need to see how you're going to move into your new job. For example, if you can walk or cycle to your current job and you can't get to the other job in any of these ways, you will have to subtract this daily cost for the days worked in order to take into account how much our real salary will be. In addition, we must add the stress that it will take us to arrive at our new workplace, we must assess whether this change of job is really worthwhile.

We have to look for a company that is close by, that is not going to overload us with work, that is to say, that we can still have a good schedule or maintain one like the one we had before and that we are not going to be stressed. It is important to take into account our quality of life, what good is it to earn more money in a new company if we go to this really crashed and this will make us sick? If we get sick, remember that we will also have to pay for this treatment. Let's evaluate these points, be honest and realistic. For example, if we could get to the company by bicycle but this would take us forty minutes, even though we get excited and say we're really going to do it, it's going to be our daily sport and this is the way to get there, we have to be honest with ourselves because otherwise we're going to end up taking taxis every day or driving, what will increase our cost in gasoline, mileage what subtracts value to the car, will increase the time in which we must do maintenance to the car because we are going to accumulate mileage faster, will increase our budget for repairs of the car, among others. This is like Monday's excuse start diet or just a potato chip and we end up eating the whole tray, so we have to keep it in mind and be really honest with ourselves. If we're going to do it every day because we're used to getting up earlier and doing sports in the perfect morning, the budget is going to be real, we can get there this way and it won't increase our expenses, but if we know there's a possibility that we can't get up earlier and that we want to drive or go by taxi, then let's not make the change.

You have decided that you do not want to change company, that you want to follow exactly where you are and that you want to get a job somewhere else, you can increase your income by looking for a part-time job, that is, you do not work a full day, full hours, but you work by the hour. There are part-time jobs where you work four hours a day, suddenly you may find one where you can work two more hours. You also have to evaluate what you do during the day, what the tasks are, if you're going to be very tired, if you'll be able to do it and the type of work you're applying for. As we have already told you, it is useless to work eight hours a day, to go to a part-time job four hours more to be able to pay our debts faster if we end up sick, if we end up stressed and most likely sick, or resign because we cannot or worse yet, that we look bad with one or both jobs because we are thinking of the other or we are very tired and stop performing in both.

That's why we really have to meditate and think about which is the best option for us. Do you want to work two hours a day and find a part-time job? Do you know that it won't affect you? Are you sure about that? Then take it and add the additional income to your budget. We will emphasize that this extra money will serve to achieve your financial freedom, not to buy you that pair of new shoes you liked or a new shirt. Put it in your emergency fund because you never know when we might have some kind of mishap.

Chapter III: Work using the digital world and market from home or anywhere in the world

Now, you've decided you don't want to spend any more time in an office, you haven't found any job you want to change to or work part-time in. Do you think you can't generate additional income unless you work in an office? That's false, welcome to the digital age. Work from home, using your computer to generate additional income.

Work from home? All jobs aren't face-to-face? No, you can generate income using only your computer and your skills. Then let's start by giving you some options on how you could generate income from your home.

Are you bilingual, trilingual? How many languages do you speak? Use languages as your added value, as a skill, take it this way and find jobs in the digital marketplace. Where? In the digital world. What do we mean by that? That on the Internet there are a variety of websites and different options and modalities to find work. For example, let's say you speak French, Spanish and English to perfection, that is, you have a good level in these languages and native in one. So, what do I do with these languages? You ask yourself. Easy, we can get text translation jobs on different web pages like Text master, Translated, One hour translation, among others. This will allow us to work as translators using the languages, we already know; we don't have to learn anything new.

These web pages allow us to work safely, from our computer and during the hours we have time, that is, if we have a week especially loaded with work in our office, that week we can decide not to do this type of work. Just like that? Yes, just like that! Register on different pages so that you are more likely to find more jobs or always have an additional job. Now, if we're going to have this additional work, don't change your budget because you don't know how much you're going to earn on a fixed basis, then, you better write down how much this income is and use it to pay off the principal on your debts, for your emergency fund or to put it in your savings account so that it generates more interest for you.

Apart from these pages, which are usually used strictly for translation work, we recommend that you also enter pages where you are looking for freelancers to work with. What is working as a freelancer? This means that you work for a company, for a person or for a project in a non-attendance way, i.e. remotely. There are companies looking for translators on this type of freelance pages. The good thing about these pages is that they regulate the entire payment process and can defend you in case there is a problem with the client or vice versa. They are very good option to find this type of work.

Now, if you speak different languages you can work as a translator, or you could start teaching one of the languages you speak. You can be a teacher online, there are many websites that are dedicated to hiring teachers to teach remotely as for example to teach English to classes. Not only can you find these websites that allow you to teach English remotely to children's classes, but you can also find other websites that are a space where people come in looking for teachers of different languages. You only have to put the languages you want to teach, a picture of yourself, a description and usually a video. You must also set the price you will charge per hour. It is really important that we take into account the market and the price of other teachers on the pages, we do not want to be very expensive because probably our potential customers will decide to hire someone cheaper than us. We must take this especially into account when we start because we need to be hired, we leave reviews, to show how many classes and how many customers we have had. People think that the more customers we have, the better we must be, this means, that they think there is a correlation between the amount of customers and the quality of our work. We should not have a very low price because people are not going to think we are very good or they will think that we are just starting.

Remember that the perception of our potential customers is really important. For this reason, we must have a competitive price, see the type of videos that other teachers have posted and sell us, we must always take into account our personal marketing when we make our description. Remember that we can also offer a free trial class so that our potential customers know us, this can serve us to hook them, to test our service.

Chapter IV: Working as a freelancer for companies or individuals

Do you not like working as a teacher? Do you feel you have no patience? Are you very shy or do you not speak any additional language? No problem, there are many more options to work freelancer and earn money apart in your extra time, from your home, from your computer and most importantly you can be your own boss. This extra money remember it will take you to financial freedom. Do you like to take pictures or are you a photographer? Sell them!

Now, we have more options. Do you like taking pictures? Start selling them on different websites. Can you sell photos on the internet? Of course, you can sell them on different websites. For example, pages like Shutterstock pay you between twenty and thirty percent per photo downloaded, this means that the better and more photos we have and send, the more chances to increase our income as more people could download our photos more times. Another page that also pays you per download is iStock Photo, they pay approximately fifteen percent for each download. Exclusive collaborators have a higher percentage, they receive between twenty-two percent and forty-five percent. Another option we offer you is Big Stock; they pay thirty percent per individual download. In addition, they will pay you thirty-eight-dollar cents royalty for the sales of customers who have paid a subscription.

These are just three of all the pages you can find that pay you for your photos. Take advantage of them! Search for photos from your previous trips, start looking for how to take good photos, you can take a quick and easy course online. All of this will help you generate more income. Always remember to take into account and see what images are popular on these pages or what type of images are missing so that you do not have so much competition. For example, if there are many photos of couples having dinner drinking wine but there are not enough photos of boyfriends, you might find a niche. Remember that you can take different photos and upload them to these pages and you will not be charged for uploading them or have to pay any maintenance to be on this page. On the contrary, the more photos you can upload to these pages the more possibilities to sell and the more people who could buy your photos.

You don't like selling photos? No problem. Evaluate your skills and start earning money with them. For example, if you like and are good at marketing in your company, use this skill and sell it online. Excuse me? For example, if you work in digital marketing in your company or have experience in this, sell it online and find projects that match your skills. If you have worked in accounting, look for clients in freelancer pages to earn extra money. It's simple. Now, if you think you don't have skills or you're not sure what they are, no problem.

On pages like Coursera you can find free courses where you can learn different skills. You don't get a degree but it comes out that you have completed the course, if you want a degree, you can pay for it and it's not expensive.

It is important that when you find a freelancer job you give a good service so that you can get recommendations. On the other hand, it is also important that you work with people who give you security. For example, check that the websites where you get work have payment policies, usually the work of the freelancer through these pages have the page as an intermediary in case they have a problem. All communication between you and the client must be through the website, the client pays to the website and once you give the advance and the client gives him the ok or give all the work and the client gives him the ok, the website pays you. This avoids fraud, not being paid, being paid late, or being paid a price that was not the one they had agreed upon.

On the other hand, it is also very important that you put a price that is within the market. Before putting our price, we must review how much people who perform a service similar to ours charge to not charge so expensive that we do not want to hire, but so cheap that they think we give a bad service or that we are not professionals.

Chapter V: Selling products on the Internet as your own brand or selling what you no longer use

Do you have a brand of clothes, accessories, hats or something else or do you simply have too many clothes in your room or things that you no longer use? Sell them and earn money! Ah? Can I sell clothes or things of mine online? Of course, you can, all you have to do is make it clear that it's second-hand, that's all and people are going to buy it. How do I do this? There are different websites where you can upload all the products you want to sell, they give you a template, you upload the photos, describe them, put the price and that's it. Now, it is very important that you analyze the competition, that is to say, that you see what the rest of the people or companies are selling on the Internet and that in this way you can have a price that is within the market. For example, let's say you have a pair of shoes that you put on once and that you no longer want to wear. You can sell them through different channels.

Let's start with pages like Amazon or eBay, here you only register as a user, you put your shoes, your policies in case they want to return them, the size of the shoes, the material, among others and you put them on sale. In this way, you would only pay the commission that the page asks you and you would not have to invest any of your money. You can also use the Facebook Marketplace, which is like a large virtual store where people can come up and sell things. Apart from that you can also search for different buying and selling groups in your city and put them there. That way, you can make quick, easy money selling items you don't use.

Also, if you want to sell products and become a company or have them on websites you can do so. Let's say you like them and you can get hats in your city, pages like Amazon, eBay and Alibaba allow the sale of products as a company and only ask for a sales commission. In other words, you wouldn't need to spend so much money to advertise and look for potential customers because these pages already have traffic of people who trust them and who want to buy products, they aren't necessarily looking for hats but if they are looking for other types of products. What you would have to do is log in and register as a company, upload your products to the templates offered by the pages, add the descriptions and then you would have to wait to see your metrics. What do we mean by that? That you should see how many people see your photos and if you're selling any. If not, what you can do in this case is advertise your product.

It is important that if you want to generate income with a separate online store create a Facebook page and Instagram for your company, we also recommend using Pinterest. You can connect the pages and you can share your products, articles or you can update and get more people to follow you. So that you don't spend so much money, we recommend you ask all your friends to put I like it, that is, to follow your page in both social networks. After this, they could also invite their friends or they can share your page on their walls so that people start following you.

It is important that the content you share is of good quality and is a topic that people may be interested in or that it is a good photo. For example, there are different websites where you can get good quality photos for free like Apixaban and Unsplashed. This makes you have professional photos but you don't pay for them. You should remember that many images, such as those in Google's search engine, are copyrighted and cannot be shared without permission from the person who took them. This is really important because you might have to pay a fine apart from downloading the photo from your social networks for infringing copyright law.

Chapter VI: Create Specialized Courses and Sell Them Online

Have you gone to college? Do you have a job in a specialized area? Have you not yet been convinced by any of these options? Are you a creative person who likes a challenge? We have more options for you to start creating money from home in order to achieve financial freedom. Start creating online courses, you can sell them on different pages to increase your income. How can we start creating our website? The first step to being able to start earning more money using your computer is to start planning this course. Start by determining what course you could teach, it could be something related to a skill you have acquired in your work, it could be something you have learned naturally or it could even be a hobby that you really know in depth and that you would love to be able to share with others.

Now that you know what course you could teach; we have to do a market analysis. A market analysis? What do we mean by that? This means that we must investigate if there are courses like these in the digital market, if people are really looking for them and most importantly, if they are willing to pay for them. Why? No matter how good we are in some field, we can build the best course we can but there is no demand, that is, people do not want to buy them. This for us is going to be a waste of energy and time. This is why it is really important to do a market analysis first. From here we can begin to take the actions we need to achieve success in our sales. Now, if you have found that people are willing to pay for the course, what you should do is start describing the course. We recommend you start planning it before it becomes more structured, there are things you should think about before you start creating it. Think about how you will deliver the course, you can think if this will be like videos, text and/or audio. This will guide you on what kind of platforms you should start using or could use for your video course. You must also take into account what your audience is.

The target audience is either beginner or advanced. It is necessary to think if later we should make additional courses, if we could have sequels or similar courses. Now that we have this information, we must choose the ideal platform for your virtual course. For example, UDEMY is a very good platform where they sell different courses. Udemy is the platform we recommend because it is a really popular market and can help us start selling our courses. It is much easier to sell them on a popular platform that people already know and trust. Because it is a popular platform, they have different filters for the courses, people who want to buy the courses feel confident because they know that the payments are secure, that they are not going to clone their credit cards and that in case they have a problem with the course they can contact a Udemy support person to help them. This generates much more confidence in the potential customers to whom you want to sell your product.

If you had a website with courses but people don't know you, you don't have many reviews, you don't have many followers, people won't trust you as much. Generate online reputation as a page of courses is complicated, so we recommend that the easiest way to generate money quickly is to find a skill that we have, create a course on a simple platform on which we can sell our product, display it so that people want to buy it. It should be a known page, that people trust you and that has a lot of people traffic. This will facilitate the sale of our course.

Once we have chosen what we are going to teach, we have carried out market research, created the course on the appropriate platform and put it on sale on pages like Udemy, we can easily create money. Remember that always the platforms you must search for to publish must be known, they must already have traffic, they must have payment method for the client and they must have a trajectory. They must be known platforms for you to have more opportunities to sell your course.

Chapter VII: How to Make Money with Virtual Coins Like Bitcoin

Bitcoin is a digital currency that is becoming very well known, this currency can be used to pay for different products on the Internet, you can buy and sell as if they were shares. Have you heard about it? Do you know what it is? This type of virtual currency, Bitcoin, is well known worldwide. We have one more proposal to be able to achieve financial freedom, it is very easy and simple, it is free and it is not laborious to get this money. Next we will explain you different activities that we can begin to realize to begin to earn money from our computer in a simple way from our house or from any part of the world. This way of making money is fast and direct, and we know how much money we are going to receive according to the type of activity carried out.

First, do you know what bitcoin is? It is a virtual currency that we can use to buy in different stores that are already accepting it as a means of payment. Is it money, does it have value? Yes, and this value is changing. How do I get this money? You may be wondering. Here are some recommendations for you to get this money. Not only can you buy it, but you can get it for free with little effort. Seriously, it's not a lie, I don't have to pay for it. No, there are ways in which you can get it for free on the internet in exchange for performing relatively simple tasks. For example, you can easily start accumulating this currency in trading operations, you can do micro tasks, you can get free coins including bitcoin taps, collect tips, you can invest in bitcoins, sell products and services in bitcoin way and more.

What do we mean by bitcoin trading? We understand that these terms are new and may seem complicated but they are not. Now, about trading, the basic speculation strategy is the one that applies, you must buy the currency when it is with the lowest price you think it could get and then you expect the price to increase to be able to sell it and this will generate a profit. How do I know what is or what will be the price of bitcoin? To know it is of utmost importance to follow the news daily to be able to negotiate with more information at hand and to be able to make wise decisions. We will not be able to know in advance how much the price is or will be, we must stay calm and check the price day by day.

Think about bitcoin as stocks, the price is going to change every day so you will have to revise them daily. Although we believe we know what will happen to this price, we must handle it day after day so we recommend reviewing this information every morning to make informed and accurate decisions. You could also make this negotiation through arbitration, buy cheap in one change and sell at a higher price in another. It is very important that before you buy or start using bitcoin you learn how it works. There are many tutorials on YouTube and a lot of information on the internet that we recommend you research before buying bitcoins.

Now, how do you earn bitcoins without having to buy them? It performs micro tasks. How do I perform micro tasks in order to earn bitcoins? Do micro tasks demand a lot of time? No, they are very simple operations and / or chores that the consumer does and that to the company that is doing it can be worth the difference between selling a product and not selling it. There are some applications where you are paid in bitcoin such as Bituro. This smartphone application pays you in bitcoins after you've done small activities like watching videos, completing surveys, testing applications, and more. These tasks don't take long, they are quite simple and help you earn virtual money. Is this true? Yes, you can go to the different pages that have this opportunity and which many of us are enjoying. These tasks can be done from your cell phone, at any time of the day, during your lunch hour at work or at night. It is very important that you want to do them, you learn to do them and you can do it yourself.

On the other hand, bitcoin reward also allows you to earn money by doing the same type of micro tasking, such as watching videos, completing surveys and other less complicated tasks inclusive. I go in to watch videos, play online games and I can make money? Yeah, and you make money. Another alternative is the hit buckszn. Coin bucks is another application you can use for Smartphone that also allows you to earn bitcoins by performing simple tasks such as playing video games, downloading other types of applications and completing online promotions. This helps companies with their market research, allows them to learn to offer different promotions to people or in this case to segment them.

How do I generate bitcoins through Bitcoin faucets? If you like to play video games, you like to watch videos and you don't mind the ads, these types of tap sites generate their ad revenue and pay a small amount of advertising revenue to their users. All you need to do is register with your bitcoin address and start earning a few bitcoin cents every day. We understand that it is a slow way to earn money but you must remember that it is free, it is simple and it adds up. Another option is also your own bitcoin tap, this will make you earn even more money. The problem is that you will have to search for good traffic on Google or other search engines, you can do this with a good website, or with Google Ads.

We can invest a little money to increase our traffic and have even more income. We must remember that both alternatives are viable, we can start with one, for example, start earning little money and then create our own website to be able to have a little more experience and understand how these websites and bitcoin work.

Still not convinced by Bitcoin? Why don't you believe in this coin yet? Do you think it won't work for you? Aren't you very sure about the value of single coins? We recommend that you go to the library or your computer and see the difference between growing up in a more technological generation or less, relying on the internet and buying things online really changes. Watch videos on

YouTube, read a bit more about the bitcoin coin, there are many pages where they explain how it works with examples and what to do to be able to succeed and win this digital coin or buy it cheaper and be able to sell it more expensive so your profits are higher. I recommend that you start by exploring and earning money on the pages where you are given Bitcoin, so that you begin to understand how Bitcoin works, where you can use this currency and how these pages work, so that later you can make a decision about which type of page is best for you.

Now that you've read all our alternatives to generate more revenue and manage your money well, it's time to increase your profits. There are different ways to increase your income. First you have to see how much you need to save or how much you need to increase your income in order to pay off your debts and achieve your financial freedom. The first option if you like your job and you like going to the office is to ask for a raise. If you're a couple of years old and you do a good job, ask for a raise. This is the easiest option for you to avoid working harder and having to have an additional worry. If your boss says yes, you shouldn't have any trouble adjusting to the previous budget but more money will help you pay off your debts or save in a savings account that gives you interest based on the amount of money in that account.

On the other hand, if you can't ask for a raise because you're very new at work, you can look for another job that pays you more taking into account your mental health as well, that is, take into account the work environment and how far away it is, if you have to travel a lot and if this is going to add stress to your day, hours of transportation and if you have to spend extra to get to work. You can also evaluate what your skills are to be able to look for an additional part-time job, you could work a couple of hours a day in another place but you must take into account that you must also rest and that if you hurry and work too many hours a day you will probably get stressed and end up getting sick for this reason. Now, if you don't want to look for a job or work somewhere else like another office, start looking for a job as a freelancer. Evaluate your skills, see what you're good at and start applying to jobs like this. For example, if you work in digital marketing, apply to community manager or digital marketing jobs in different companies and work remotely.

Many websites have a digital job market and sporadically look for people to complete jobs. Log in, sign up and start looking for a job. You will have to complete your profile and put a price for your work. We recommend that you do this on websites that are known to you and that you read reviews of these pages first. Now, if you don't like working as a freelancer or think you don't have any specific skills, you can take courses on the internet with websites like Coursera, they offer free courses and this will allow you to develop different skills and you can work online. Alternatively, if you speak different languages, look for work remotely, i.e. online, as a translator or teacher of these languages. There are different pages where you can work remotely for institutions, for example, that teach English, you choose your schedule and you get paid monthly.

Now, you can also sign up for different websites that are for private teachers who teach languages via video. Research these options and see if any of them are for you. Didn't like any of the options? Start selling your photos online! Many websites buy photos so they can sell them on their site and this allows you to get a commission every time someone downloads your photos, even can give you royalties. Not thinking about selling your photos? Create an online course and sell it on websites like Udemy. Just look for a platform, create it and you're done. These are just some of the options you will find in the digital market that allows you to work from home, from your computer and generate extra income. This will allow you to get financial freedom and more income quickly and easily. All of these suggested changes will not only change our routine, they will also change our mentality and our relationship and understanding of our finances and our money. It will help us save and this will be simpler than we have always believed, we will be able to reach our goals and achieve financial freedom, we will learn and regain control of our money and time. These small changes in our daily routine will help us reach our financial goals, pay our debts and have our emergency fund.

We shouldn't be stressed about money; we should have better handling. We don't necessarily need that increase or additional work, we must learn to reduce and minimize the additional luxury expenses we have and we must learn to make rational, conscious, planned and unemotional decisions. Start today and change your life! Save today!

Chapter VIII: How to achieve financial freedom at age 40?

We all want to reach this goal, be it at 40, at 50, and why not, at 35... that's why we will now focus on mentioning 5 key points for you to work on your goal of achieving financial freedom at the earliest possible age.

1. Be free to decide

Decide how you want to live your life when you grow up. You'd like to work office hours, or you don't want that for yourself. Likewise, you don't want to depend on someone who constantly tells you what to do. Changing the way, you live is your decision and it's the most important thing.

2. Don't misinterpret the term wealth

The concept of wealth is associated with a very high level of income and with owning property. It's a mistake to associate financial freedom with this idea in your mind. It incorporates a new vision in which time, not money, is the determining factor to increase your economic freedom.

3. Focus on what's important

Focusing on how much you spend rather than how much you earn is what's important. It is no longer a matter of dedicating your life to work but of reducing your efforts to correctly manage your income. Manage your emotions and see what you spend on. Watch your cash flow.

If you save 30% of your salary by limiting your expenses such as not buying a luxurious car, not eating out all the time or constantly and not having ant expenses, which are very dangerous in the long term, among others, you will achieve it.

4. Work for and with pleasure

If you save you will be able to work in what you like, in what makes you happy, since you will not do it for hours nor for money but you will work for satisfaction, and as many hours as you wish in the week. In other words, it is not a question of stopping working completely, but rather, by saving enough capital, you will only need a part of what you earned before and dedicate the rest of your day to what you imagined.

5. Looking for an active income

Having active income, or money from sources that don't require regular work, is an excellent idea and a great challenge. You can write practical books, interesting blogs, generate real estate rentals, etc.

It's important to keep in mind that any one month of that income could go away, although it's also unlikely to go to zero overnight. It's not about accumulating interest over time but getting enough to save day after day.

Chapter IX: It's a matter of attitude

Creating budgets, saving money and getting out of debt is also a matter of attitude. Why do we say this? Because we must want to do it in order to do it! No matter how much we want not to have debts or get out of them, but we mentalize ourselves, make the plan, follow it and change it, it is going to be impossible for us to achieve financial freedom. Remember that all change must come from you. We can guide you and explain how to create budgets, we can recommend which expenses to cut but in the end, it will depend on you to think and achieve freedom. You will see the quantity of benefits and the quality of life that this financial freedom will give you. Remember that the road is not going to be easy, having budgets is difficult and getting jobs on the internet too. If you don't get the first job you're looking for, don't get discouraged, it's always like that, we just have to keep looking and keep applying to different jobs online. Don't get discouraged because nothing's easy.

On the other hand, you're going to need to be motivated to be able to do the extra work and you're going to need to get better organized. We recommend that you use a diary or plan your day, this way, you will be more productive, you will be able to organize yourself in a better way, you will not have so much stress by the additional workload and you will not lose your goal that is the financial freedom. Always keep in mind what you want to achieve, why you are doing this extra work and the fruits it will bring to your life.

If we want to be successful in life, we must learn how to overcome difficult situations and we must always be positive and optimistic. Follow our advice and get rid of your debts, get financial freedom, save more money, even if you want to invest more money to earn more. Take risks but always keep in mind what your goal is. Never forget that reaching our goals is not in straight lines, we will always have to try new things, get out of our comfort zone, we will fail sometimes but more importantly, we will succeed. Begin with this journey to financial freedom, read this book as many times as necessary, take it with you as well as your goals and your reasons. With determination you can achieve what you want, aim for financial freedom, follow your budget, get extra money in any of the ways already explained, and get ready to live in absolute freedom.

Bibliography

Andres N, A. N. (2019, 14 February). Work as a translator - MeVoyalMundo. Recovered October 13, 2019, from https://mevoyalmundo.com/trabajar-como-traductor/

Diego Ortiz, D. O. (2019, October 8). 20 online jobs you can start today without money. Recovered October 13, 2019, from https://www.emprendiendohistorias.com/trabajos-online-ganar-dinero/

20 Internet Jobs ? that you can start TODAY! (2019, 29 June). Recovered October 13, 2019, from https://carlicas.com/trabajos-por-internet/

www.ingramcontent.com/pod-product-compliance
Lightning Source LLC
Chambersburg PA
CBHW071522210326
41597CB00018B/2860